W9-BKK-084

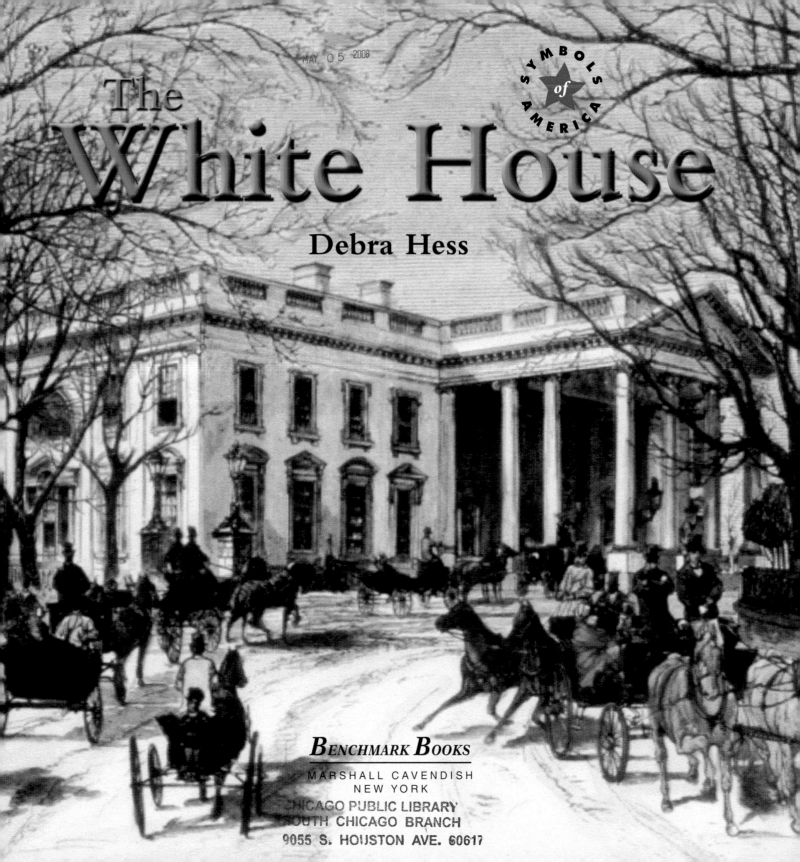

SYMBOLS of AMERICA

The White House

Debra Hess

BENCHMARK BOOKS

MARSHALL CAVENDISH
NEW YORK

Benchmark Books
Marshall Cavendish
99 White Plains Road
Tarrytown, NY 10591-9001
www.marshallcavendish.com

Library of Congress Cataloging-in-Publication Data

Hess, Debra.
  The White House / by Debra Hess.
      p. cm.—(Symbols of America)
Summary: Traces the history of the White House, including its construction, repairs and renovations through the years, uses, and what it means to Americans today.
Includes bibliographical references (p.) and index.
  ISBN 0–7614–1712–5
  1. White House (Washington, D.C.)—Juvenile literature. 2. Washington (D.C.)—Buildings, structures, etc.—Juvenile literature. 3. Presidents—United States—Juvenile literature. [1. White House (Washington, D.C.) 2. Philadelphia (Pa.)—Buildings, structures, etc. 3. Presidents.] I. Title. II. Series: Hess, Debra. Symbols of America.

F204.W5H47 2004
975.3—dc21
                                        2003004462
Photo research by Anne Burns Images

Front cover: Corbis/Craig Aurnesse
Back cover: Corbis/Richard T. Nowitz

The photographs in this book are used by permission and through the courtesy of:
North Wind Pictures: title page. *Corbis:* Adam Woolfitt, 4; Wally McNamee, 7; Corbis, 11 (bottom); Lester Lefkowitz, 35.
The Granger Collection: 8, 9 (top), 15, 16, 20, 24, 27, 28, 31. *Photri-Microstock:* 12, 19, 23, 32.

Series design by Adam Mietlowski

Printed in Italy

1 3 5 6 4 2

Contents

CHAPTER ONE

A Home for the President

The president of the United States of America lives in a large *mansion* in Washington, D.C. It is called the White House, and it is one of the most famous buildings in America. Although it is the home of our nation's president, it is open to everyone. Americans from across the country and people from all over the world visit the White House. Every year more than one million visitors come to the White House. They walk through the many rooms and halls that are open to the public. Along the way, they learn how past presidents and *first ladies* have lived in a house that has become a symbol of America throughout the world.

◄ *The White House—a symbol of the president as well as the nation*

Visitors who take tours of the White House will probably not meet the president. He works in the Oval Office in the West Wing of the house. He lives with his family on the top floor. To respect the president's privacy, this space is off-limits to the public. To see the president in his office, you have to make an appointment.

The White House was built more than 200 years ago. Although some changes have been made, today the general shape and structure of the White House are the same as in November 1800 when John Adams (who served from 1797 to 1801), the second president, first moved in.

The Oval Office is where the president helps run the nation. ▶

1791

In 1789 George Washington (who served from 1789 to 1797) became the first president of the United States. One year later, Congress voted that there should be *permanent* homes for not only the president, but Congress and the Supreme Court as well. They chose the shores of the Potomac River as the site of the nation's capital. In 1800 Congress ordered the federal government to move from Philadelphia to a new city that they would name Washington, D.C. The D.C. stands for District of Columbia, which is part of the city's official name.

A French *architect* named Pierre L'Enfant mapped the city streets of Washington, D.C. The city would cover 10 square miles (26 square kilometers) of what had once been farmland. George Washington was asked to choose the spot for the president's house. L'Enfant set aside space for what he called "a palace for the president."

◀ *President George Washington, on horseback, talks to Pierre L'Enfant about his plans for the nation's new capital city.*

Officials wondered, what should the house look like? Who would design it? Secretary of State Thomas Jefferson came up with the best solution. He announced a contest for architects and builders to enter their designs for the president's new house. He placed an advertisement in newspapers. The winner would choose a prize of $500 or a medal of the same value. Many designers entered the *competition*. James Hoban, a builder from Ireland who was working in Charleston, South Carolina, was named the winner.

Hoban drew up a plan in 1792. The plan included a first floor, or "state" floor, where public business would be *conducted*. Hoban created rooms of different sizes and shapes. Most of the rooms would be used for holding *receptions* and serving dinners to guests. The president's family would live on the second floor.

James Hoban (top) worked for many months on his floor plans (bottom) for the White House.

Private
Telgh
Room

President's
Office

Cabinet
Room

Library

Bed
Chamber

Bed
Chamber

Dressing Room

Waiting Room

Clerk

Hall

Reception

Private
Office

Secretary
to the
President

Guest
Chamber

House-keeper

Guest
Chamber

Elevator

Bath
Room

Guest
Chamber

Dressing Room

·SECOND·STORY·
·PLAN·

·SHOWING·

·EXECUTIVE·OFFICES·
·AND·PRESIDENTS·FAMILY·
·APARTMENTS·

James Hoban, Archt. 1792.

F. D. Owen. del.
Copyrighted 1901.

Hoban's original design had two stories and a raised *basement*, but some thought the house was too large. Others wondered whether enough quality sandstone could be collected to build such a large house. Stone was also needed to build the U.S. Capitol, where Congress would meet. So George Washington agreed that the president's house could be only two stories. The idea of the raised basement would be dropped from the design. Washington knew that the design they finally settled on would allow future presidents to make additions if they needed more space.

◀ *The White House was designed so that it could be changed in order to fit the needs of future leaders. More than two hundred years later, it is still an impressive sight.*

Hoban was to be in charge of building the house. The *cornerstone* was laid on October 13, 1792. *Stonemasons* from Scotland, along with free laborers and hired slaves, worked on the building from spring through fall—it was too cold in the winter—for the next eight years. By that time America had a new president. George Washington never even had the chance to live in the White House. It was President John Adams and his wife, Abigail, who moved into the new building.

This is how the White House looked in 1799, just before the Adamses were ready to move in. ▶

CHAPTER TWO

Living in the White House

When John and Abigail Adams moved into the White House in 1800, it was not yet finished. Many of the plaster walls were still wet, and fires were lit in several of the thirty-nine fireplaces to help the walls dry. About half of the thirty-six rooms had not been plastered at all. There was a big hole where the grand staircase was planned, but not yet begun. The largest room in the house, the East Room, was also unfinished. Because Abigail Adams thought that the president's laundry should not be hung outside to dry on the lawn where everyone could see, she set up clotheslines in the East Room.

◀ *Though the basic structure of the White House was finished in 1800, there was still much work to be done on the inside.*

Later, Americans were invited to the mansion for public receptions. People had the chance to meet the president, enjoy cake and lemonade with the first lady, dance, chat, and even wander through the rooms and grounds. But times changed, and the Adamses began to host very formal receptions. President Adams invited only certain gentlemen to afternoon affairs called levees. He would bow to them and say just a few words. When all the gentlemen had been greeted, Adams would bow once again, and the guests would depart.

In the evenings, Abigail Adams would hold a less formal reception. Men and women arrived without a formal invitation, but they were expected to dress and act in a proper manner. They drank tea, coffee, wine, or cold punch and ate small cakes and fruit. From time to time, President Adams would invite guests to dinner.

Through the years, the White House has been the site of many elegant receptions. Here, the Blue Room displays a portrait of the man who started it all, President John Adams (left).

The third president, Thomas Jefferson (who served from 1801 to 1809), was the first American leader to spend his entire term in the White House. An architect himself, Jefferson designed two long wings that stretched to the east and west. These wings added office and storage space.

Each president who has lived in the White House has made additions to the building and changed the way it looks on the inside. But thanks to wise planning, the White House still looks much as it did when it was first built.

Did You Know?

A president's *inauguration* used to be an opportunity for citizens to visit the White House. When Andrew Jackson (who served from 1829 to 1837) was sworn in as the seventh president in 1829, a mob of people forced their way into the White House. They stood on the furniture with muddy boots and pushed their way through the rooms. Dozens of glasses, cups, and plates were broken. The new president escaped and spent the night in a nearby hotel. Hardly anyone noticed that he had left! The crowd spilled out onto the lawn and continued to drink punch from large tubs.

Not only a strong leader, Thomas Jefferson was a talented architect as well. He made several key changes to the president's official home.

When the British set fire to the White House on August 24, 1814, during the War of 1812, James Madison (who served from 1809 to 1817) and his wife, Dolley, escaped capture. After the fire, some members of Congress suggested rebuilding the president's house in another place, perhaps in another city. But President Madison wanted Americans to know that the British *invasion* was not a serious threat to the capital. By making the White House appear exactly as it did before the war, it would *symbolize* America's *determination* to survive. It would show that the nation and its government were permanent.

The British burned the White House during the War of 1812. Dolley Madison was able to save a valuable portrait of George Washington as she ran from the building. ▶

When *engineers* examined the building in 1814, they saw that the floors and inside walls had been destroyed. But parts of the *exterior* stone walls were strong enough to use again. To make sure that the construction was done properly, James Hoban was hired to rebuild the president's house. No one knew the building better than Hoban, since he was the original designer.

The house was ready in 1817 for America's fifth president, James Monroe (who served from 1817 to 1825). After the rebuilding and repairs, the White House did not change until the beginning of the 1900s, when porches were added to the north and south sides.

◀ *President James Monroe poses in the newly restored White House.*

CHAPTER THREE

The Twentieth Century and Beyond

When Theodore Roosevelt (who served from 1901 to 1909) was sworn in as the twenty-sixth president, he was the youngest man to have held the office. At forty-two years old, Roosevelt brought a wife and six children to the White House. Things became quickly crowded. Privacy was an issue as well. Although the Roosevelt family lived on the second floor, anyone who had business with the president would walk upstairs to his office. Throughout the day, strangers would be only a room away from the president's family.

President Theodore Roosevelt in the White House in 1903. A large family living there meant more changes to the building were on the way. ▶

President Theodore Roosevelt decided to move not only his office but the offices of his *cabinet* and staff from the second floor of the White House to a new West Wing. He ordered it to be built in 1902. Now the entire second floor could be used for the president's family. To build the West Wing, large greenhouses would have to be taken down. For years they had been home to the flowers and potted plants that were grown to decorate the White House. Roosevelt ordered, "Smash the glass houses!" He also added a new east entrance to the grounds. It was big enough to allow large groups to enter in their carriages.

◀ *A rare look at the White House greenhouses. To build the new West Wing, they had to be torn down.*

By the middle of the 1900s, dozens of smaller *renovations* and additions had weakened the White House. The floors were in danger of collapsing. In 1948 President Harry Truman (who served from 1945 to 1953) wrote that, in his daughter Margaret's second-floor bedroom, the leg of her piano had fallen through the floor. The impact knocked parts of the ceiling loose in the family dining room below. Sometimes President Truman would also notice that chandeliers in the Blue Room and the East Room swayed back and forth. No one could explain why.

The East Room was once the site of lavish state dinners. By the late 1940s, though, President Harry Truman noticed the lights were swinging loosely overhead. Major repairs were needed. ▶

President Harry Truman asked engineers and architects to examine the White House. They found that the house needed a lot of work in order to save it. The outer walls—the same walls that James Hoban had built—could be saved. But the entire interior had to be removed. Bulldozers were used to create more basement space. This provided more storage room and areas for heating and air-conditioning equipment. The White House was also fireproofed. The size and shape of many of the rooms were changed to try and match the building's original plans. All of this work took four years to complete. During this time, the Truman family moved across the street to Blair House, a government building where officials sometimes stayed.

◀ *President Harry Truman knew the importance of preserving this important American symbol.*

In 1952 the work was done, and the Truman family moved back into the White House. The building was stronger, safer, and ready to serve the nation's leaders for years to come. The look of the president's home has not changed since.

Each president and his family have decorated the White House as they liked. They have also entertained in their own way and favored one room or another in which to spend their time at business or play. But each president has understood that from the outside the look of the building must remain the same. That is because the White House is home to the leader of the United States of America. It is part of American history and one of the nation's most important buildings. Across the country, people look to the White House as a symbol of freedom and liberty for all.

Today the official address of the White House is 1600 Pennsylvania Avenue. It sits on 18 acres of gardens and lawns.

Glossary

architect—Someone who designs buildings.

basement—An area or room below the ground floor in a building.

cabinet—A group of advisors to the president.

competition—A contest.

conduct—To carry out.

cornerstone—A stone placed where two sides of a building meet.

determination—Not giving up, staying focused on achieving a goal.

engineer—Someone who is trained to design and build structures.

exterior—The outside or outer part of something.

first lady—The president's wife.

inauguration—The ceremony to swear in a newly elected official.

invasion—An attack by soldiers sent into another country in order to take it over.

mansion—A large house.

permanent—Lasting.

reception—A formal social gathering.

renovation—A change or improvement to a building.

stonemason—Someone who is skilled in working with stone.

symbolize—To stand for or represent.

Find Out More

Books

Binns, Tristan Boyer. *The White House*. Crystal Lake, IL: Heinemann
    Library, 2001.

Feinberg, Barbara Silberdick. *The Changing White House*. Danbury,
    CT: Children's Press, 2000.

Sanders, Mark C. *The White House*. Austin, TX: Raintree/Steck-
    Vaughn, 2001.

Web Sites

Children in the White House
http://clinton4.nara.gov/WH/kids/html/children.html

History of the White House Easter Egg Roll
http://clinton4.nara.gov/WH/glimpse/Easter/

The White House
http://www.surfnetkids.com/whitehouse.htm

The White House Historical Association Learning Center
http://www.whitehousehistory.org/02_learning/02_learning_b.html

White House Kids
http://www.whitehouse.gov/kids

Index